Faithbuilders Publishing

A Garland of Grace

by Doreen Harrison

A Garland of Grace by Doreen Harrison

First Published in Great Britain in 2016

FAITHBUILDERS PUBLISHING www.biblestudiesonline.org.uk

An Imprint of Apostolos Publishing Ltd,

3rd Floor, 207 Regent Street,

London W1B 3HH

www.apostolos-publishing.com

Copyright © 2016 Doreen Harrison

All rights reserved. No part of this book may be reproduced or transmitted in any form or by any means, electronic or mechanical, including photocopying, recording, or by any information storage and retrieval system, without permission in writing from the publisher.

Unless otherwise indicated, all scripture quotations in this publication are from the Good News Translation in Today's English Version- Second Edition Copyright © 1992 by American Bible Society. Used by Permission.

Scripture quotations marked "ESV" are from The Holy Bible, English Standard Version, copyright ©2001 by Crossway Bibles, a publishing ministry of Good News Publishers. Used by permission. All rights reserved.

British Library Cataloguing-in-Publication Data

A catalogue record for this book is available from the British Library

ISBN: 978-1-910942-36-9

Cover Design by Blitz Media, Pontypool, Torfaen

Cover Image © Maximus Vonet| Dreamstime Stock Photos.

Other stock photo illustrations used under license and are credited throughout.

Printed and bound in Great Britain by Marston Book Services Limited, Oxfordshire.

Dedicated to all those who (like me) are of senior years.

By the same author: A Bouquet of Blessings, The Donkey Boy, Jubilant Jeremy Johnson, A Book of Bible Stories, Coping with the Wobbles of Life.

Contents

- You are not Insignificant 8
- School Reunion 10
- You Silly Goat! 12
- Safe in His Hands 14
- Today, Tomorrow and Telephones! 16
- It's Pindonna! 18
- Look to the Heavens 20
- The Good Samaritan 22
- A Perfect Seven 24
- Surplus to Requirements? 26
- This Soap is Good! 28
- Easter Egg Time 32
- Remember Jesus 34
- My Childhood Dreams 37
- The Squirrels in our Garden 38
- Autumn Leaves 40
- Thanksgiving 42
- Glorious Mud 44
- Bring on the Rain 46
- Christmas Joy 48
- Chinese Whispers 50
- The Birthday Cake 52
- Popping Corks 54
- Garden Wildlife 56
- The Wet Sunshine 58

Keep the Rules	60
What's in a Name?	62
The Old Watch	64
The Majesty of God	66
Big Mouth!	68
Traffic Jam!	70
Rejoice and be Glad!	72
Childhood Memory	73

This book is a sequel to "A Bouquet of Blessings." It contains anecdotes, stories, thoughts which will hold you together when situations and circumstances are causing you to fall apart. It is a book for a bedside table, a coffee table, for a birthday gift, for a sick friend. It will fit into an A5 envelope. There are blessings in its pages, gathered through a life of variety and events which all underline the truth that Jesus saves, keeps—and satisfies—always and for ever.

You are not Insignificant

I am a small lady. When I was growing up in the industrial north of England I would often hear my elderly aunts discussing various older people and they would use this description: "She's getting on a bit, tha' knows—she takes up less room these days!" Age, it appeared, was indicated less by grey hair and wrinkles than by reduction in height.

Having reduced in my own height, my birth date and that description begins to tally! Certainly, now, I am a smaller lady than I was! There are certain occasions when someone looks down at me and says "Oh—I didn't see you there!"

When I was teaching in Primary school my height was an asset. I could look my pupils in the eye without bending down. I could arrange my classroom for their maximum benefit because I saw things at their level. Tall, strong 11 year old boys felt important when I enlisted their help to reach things down for their little leader! Whoever, and however you are—use what you have and enjoy each experience!

A philosopher presented an accolade for all humanity when he proclaimed, "we are marked by majesty." Each of us has a DNA containing 3 BILLION base pairs. If these very miniscule characters were placed end to end they would reach 6 feet in length.

Did you know that every cell in the human body is held in place by a protein molecule named Laminin which amazingly is shaped like a cross? Our completeness is protected by a cross; we exist in our majesty of presentation by reason of a cross. The Bible explains, *"The LORD watches over those who obey him, those who trust in his constant love. He saves them from death; he keeps them alive in times of famine."* (Psalm 33:18–19)

It is no small thing to identify His true majesty and pray: *"May your constant love be with us, LORD, as we put our hope in you."* (Psalm 33:22)

However small you are—in stature, in social significance, in success, or in stamina, God loves YOU! Such is the unalterable size of His amazing grace.

School Reunion

We have just appreciated a week away, which presented us with many contrasting experiences. We were guests at a wedding, and guests at a reunion of classmates who were at school together 50 years ago! We saw and heard swallows, just back from their migratory journey. We revisited familiar places, enjoyed meeting friendly people and ate fascinating food. One event struck a chord of special memory.

It was early evening. The main door of the place where we were staying opened and a long line of children trooped out to their waiting coach. Each child carried a yellow balloon on a stick. It was a happy end to a school outing and now they were going home. Last in line was the teacher in charge, making sure that everyone got safely on board.

I remembered a school outing, years ago, when our coach stopped for a toilet break. I stood in the doorway and asked, "Is everybody out?" I repeated the question and, as no one replied, I got on the coach.

The driver set off again. We were just about to turn onto the motorway when someone yelled, "Miss! Mary isn't here!" The driver slammed on his brakes, I did a quick head count - and, indeed, Mary wasn't with us. We returned to the service station. I shouted, "Mary! Are you there?" A door opened and Mary ran out. "Mary," I asked. "Why didn't you answer the first time I called?" She looked at me in surprise. "You said Is everybody out?" she replied. "But I'm not everybody. I'm Mary!"

Of course! We are all bound up together in the bundle of life, but that does not alter the fact that each one of us is a unique human being. The Bible records these words, spoken by God: "Israel, the LORD who created you says, *"Do not be afraid—I will save you. I have called you by name—you are mine"* (Isaiah 43:1). You are one among the trillions of people here on earth- past, present and future—but God knows you by name and to him, you are one special person.

Life is like that school journey, a learning process at the end of which we will go home! The Priest, the Pastor, the Minister are here to make sure we are in the right line and not left behind. Please appreciate that God knows your name and intends you to travel home to Him. Enjoy the journey!

You Silly Goat!

There is a derogative saying we attach to people who make obvious mistakes—"You silly goat!" I heard a story about two goats who met on a very narrow path above a steep, water filled ravine. They couldn't turn back and they couldn't pass each other. To advance for a head on collision would send both of them to their death in the water below. So what did they do? Inevitably, one goat lay down and the other goat walked over him, going safety on his way. The other goat got up and continued on his chosen path. Both achieved their purpose. No silly goats here!

But which goat gives the other first right of way? The Bible admonishes us to love our neighbour just as ourselves However, our neighbour is not always loveable! In the story, the two goats they were going in opposite directions. So in society, in politics, in countries and in families—how can diametrically opposed opinions ever be resolved without conflict? Wisdom is seldom predictable. Neither is love!

Consider the impasse in the following story featuring King Solomon, to whom *"God gave… unusual wisdom and insight, and knowledge too great to be measured"* (1Kings 4:29). Two ladies came to him to solve an argument. They both had babies, but one baby had died in the night. The mother of the dead baby took the tiny corpse and exchanged it for the living baby. Now both were laying claim to the living child.

King Solomon asked for a sword. He said, "Cut the living child in half and give each woman half of the child." The woman who was the real mother cried out, "O my Lord, give her the child, let him live!" But the other woman said, "Alright! Divide him!" Solomon rightly discerned that the woman who was willing to lose her son in order for him to live was the real mother—and at once ordered the child should not be harmed.

One lady was willing to lay down her rights and let the other woman walk right over her—carrying the baby! Willingness to give in for the sake of someone else achieved a great result. A proverb from that wise King states, *"The start of an argument is like the first break in a dam; stop it before it goes any further"* (Proverbs 17:14). Giving in gracefully achieves glorious results. Care to try it for yourself?

© R. Gino Santa Maria / Shutterfree, Llc Dreamstime.com

Safe in His Hands

Hands are articulate. They express age, experience, emotion, personality—all without words. We speak with our hands, in tender touches, soothing strokes, approval by applause, and by restraining from dangerous situations. Sign language engages conversation by gestures and movements. I have an elderly neighbour whose hands, twisted as they are with arthritis, speak of years of gracious caring for family and friends in spite of pain.

I remember, with some emotion, a 5 year old pupil who clutched my hand and explained, "When my hand fits into yours I feel so safe!"—surely an action which spoke louder than words!

I am grateful that Jesus was a carpenter. He had useful hands, hardworking hands, hands that enjoyed the texture of the wood he used in his trade, hands that cringed from hammer blows as he was nailed to the cross.

These days people wear protective gloves for all sorts of reasons. Jesus had human hands, he was not protected from any aspect of human experience and with his hands he spoke the love of God for all humanity.

There is a song with these words "He's got the whole world in his hands." Planet earth is round, like a ball. We can estimate its size and speed and compare it with the vast universes which surround it. The presentation, that God holds Earth in his hands, like a small ball, increases our awareness of His power, patience, majesty. And, of course, He never drops that ball! Consider these Bible verses:

"God has always been your defence; his eternal arms are your support" (Deuteronomy 33:27). *"You, LORD, are all I have, and you give me all I need; my future is in your hands."* (Psalm 16:5)

May I suggest a way to cope with anxiety? Gently roll a ball in your hands. Remember the song, "He's got the whole world in His hands." Then identify with these words from the Bible: *"Yet I always stay close to you, and you hold me by the hand"* (Psalm 73:23).

As the small child said, "When my hand fits into yours I feel so safe." That is an accurate description of faith!

Today, Tomorrow and Telephones!

My granddaughter carries, in the palm of her hand, a mobile phone; which also provides Google, music, Sat Nav directions and facility to Skype with her older brother in Amsterdam. Red telephone kiosks are museum pieces and land-line communication is losing out to mobile.

I recollect with amazement how I would visit an Aunt, when I was my granddaughter's age, and listen to her describe her work situation; she was a telephonist, the lady with the plumy voice who asked, "Number please!" The escalation of progress in my life time is incredible. However, not every aspect of social progress is successful. For instance, every day I meet, or hear about, someone who has succumbed to a lingering cough and cold in spite of the impact of this year's flu jab! We are grateful for progress, but real values are not always the most recent ones!

2000 years ago St Paul wrote, *"I've learned to be content in whatever situation I'm in"* (Phil. 4:11 ISV). There is delightful advice in the Bible: *"Go ahead—eat your food and be happy; drink your wine and be cheerful. It's all right with God"* (Ecclesiastes 9:7).

When my granddaughter reaches my present age, will she regard her smart phone with the amusement with which I remember the coin slot and the cultured voice of early telephones and operators? Whatever the discoveries of medical science in years to come—if you sneezed and wheezed, in spite of flu jabs, you were still here to tell the tale!

The Old Codgers, in a newspaper of bygone days, presented their items with these words "Yesterday has gone. Tomorrow has yet to come. Today is yours!"

The Bible declares, *"After all this, there is only one thing to say: Have reverence for God, and obey his commands, because this is all that we were created for"* (Ecclesiastes 12:13).

This is the day that the Lord has made—we will rejoice and be glad in it!

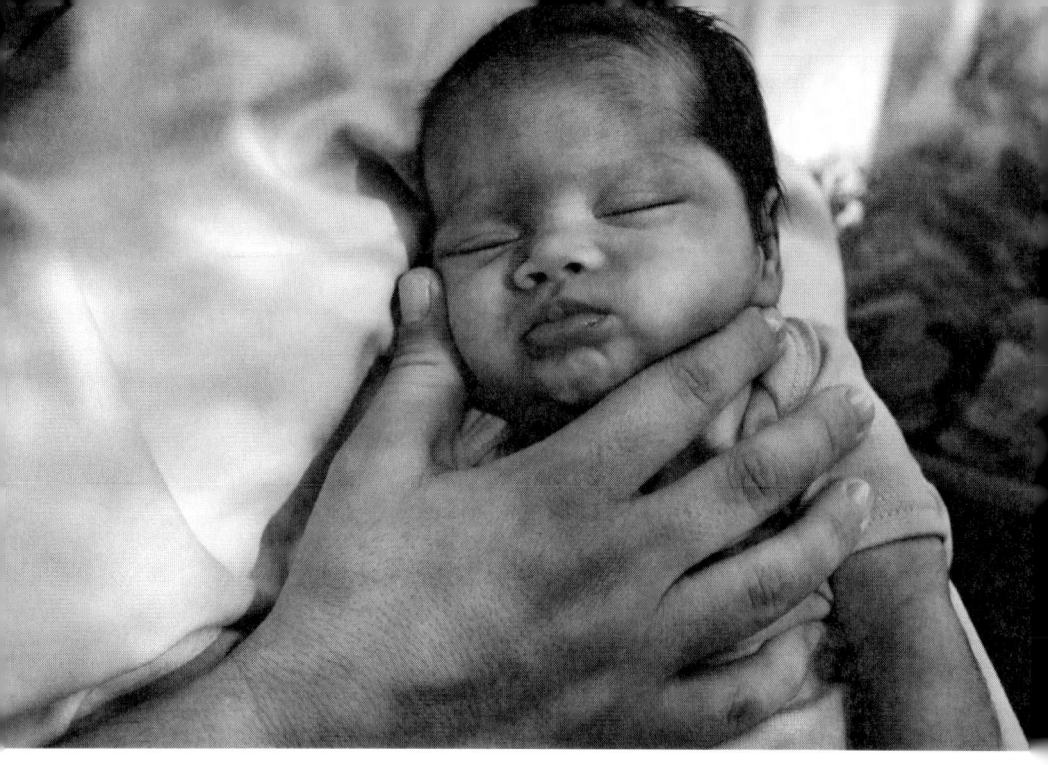

It's Pindonna!

Family gatherings are important—christenings, weddings, funerals—all are key events when everyone is there. A christening is very special. Here is a new member of the clan being blessed in the name of the Father, the Son and the Holy Spirit, protected with prayer, and identified with a name which has been chosen with care and which carries meaning, tradition, and anticipation. How many Richards achieve the stamina of a Lion Heart?

I read about a christening at which the chosen name caused some consternation. The Vicar asked, "What is this child's name?" and received the answer, "It's Pindonna!" He was well accustomed to unusual names, but this was a new one to him, so he asked again—and received the same answer, "It's Pindonna." The anxious mother noted his expression, and pointed-to a label, pinned on the babies shawl on which was written a normal and delightful name.' She said, slowly and clearly, "It is pinned on her!" and the ceremony proceeded!

I remember the Bible story of John the Baptist and his naming ceremony. Safety pins had not been invented 2000 years ago, so when there was confusion about his name, his father, Zechariah the priest, wrote his name on a piece of paper to make sure that his baby son got the name selected for him. John was special. His birth was announced by an angel who charged Zechariah, "You are to give him the name, John."

In God's eyes every child is special. Each child is a trust from God and when the family gather together for the naming ceremony, whatever form it takes, we need to identify completely with the prayers and promises made and make sure that God's plan and purpose for this new life is not neglected. The Bible affirms *"When my bones were being formed, carefully put together in my mother's womb, when I was growing there in secret, you knew that I was there—you saw me before I was born. The days allotted to me had all been recorded in your book, before any of them ever began"* (Psalm 139:15–16).

The church in which the ceremony took place will have a Sunday school to help you understand God's love for you all.

Look to the Heavens

My daughter is about to begin a teaching job in a rural school on the outskirts of Bristol. We all drove over to see where she was going to work. It was an old building, well maintained and with a playground stocked with modern equipment—including two play houses. Outside the main entrance were stone troughs overwhelmed with scarlet geraniums and trails of blue lobelia.

"Look through this window, into my classroom," said my daughter. As we clustered around the high arched window the age of the school became obvious. Being less than five feet tall, I couldn't see over the window sill! In those distant years, children went to school to be taught! Windows were made to be high so that outside views did not distract them. This is probably why the 1933 syllabus contained the sentient advice,

"If all else fails direct the pupils attention to the panoply of the sky." That was all they could see.

Recently we visited an ancient abbey. The guide book waxed eloquent about the windows, once filled with coloured glass which patterned the aisles and pillars with a multitude of crimson, orange, blue, and mauve hues when the sun shone through. The outside light transformed the inside scene. Now the windows were outlined with stone frames and arches but they still let the light in! Then that observation was affirmed in a delightful way.

An elderly lady in a wheel chair was pushed by another woman with a young boy, to the front of a church building. The boy jumped onto the flat, tiled base where the high altar had been and said, "Now I'm in the right place to pray for grandma." The light streamed through the window frames and he was praying in a pool of sunshine. Outside light really does transform a situation!

Jesus said, *"I am the light of the world"* (John 8:12). He came from outside time into the inside of human life on planet earth The Bible describes his coming like this: *"The Word became a human being and, full of grace and truth, lived among us. We saw his glory, the glory which he received as the Father's only Son."* (John 1:14)

If all else fails-direct your attention to the panoply of the sky. Let God's light shine into your heart.

The Good Samaritan

The story of The Good Samaritan is well known. If someone calls us a 'Good Samaritan' we are affirmed, even proud. But think of the story. There was a man who was travelling from Jerusalem to Jericho and he fell into the hands of robbers who took all that he had—even his clothes—and left him, half dead. How foolish he was, to take that robber-infested route on his own!

What about the robbers? They were evil men who had no pity, compassion or consideration for anyone but themselves. There was a Priest, and also a Levite, both of whom passed by on the other side! How very unprofessional! Their code of practice meant that they would be unclean if they touched a dead body—how close to death was the unfortunate traveller? They felt it was better to be safe and keep clear of that particular problem. Then a Samaritan came along; the fact that he is described as a Good Samaritan deserves a quantity of exclamation marks!!!! However else a Samaritan was described by a Jew, the adjective "good" would not normally be used. Foolish, evil, selfish, of bad reputation—this is quite a collection of negative descriptions for the characters in the famous story.

However, these characters have one thing in common. They are not named! Take note that this story is told by Jesus, who always sees the best in people. He defines the particular problems but he does not name them or allow them to be defamed. This courtesy of Jesus is the reason why this story is considered to be based on an actual event.

The Bible advises, "Do not use harmful words, but only helpful words, the kind that build up and provide what is needed, so that what you say will do good to those who hear you" (Ephesians 4:29).

I have a four-fold response to this story: 1. Don't gossip 2. Don't be judgemental 3. Don't jump to conclusions and of course 4. Love your neighbour as you love yourself.

The story was told to answer the question, "Who is my neighbour?" One derogatory modern response stated: "I do not love the human race—I do not love its silly face!" What an unfortunate comment when we are all bound up in the bundle of life together!

A Perfect Seven

I want to share some pithy comments which arrived inside a recent card. I have chosen 7 of them—7 being known as the perfect number. The first one:

> "The true test of our character is what we do when no one is looking."

I am reminded of a school cleaner that I met one evening, on her hands and knees, scrubbing in a room which was seldom used. "Isn't it time you went home?" I asked. She looks at me with surprise, "I haven't finished my work!" she explained "But whoever is going to use this room? I asked. She smiled. "Suppose the Queen pops in tomorrow? We need to be prepared for everything!" she said. Top marks for that lady! The second comment is:

> "Often the best comfort is just being there."

I was 15 when my Dad died. It was an unexpected tragedy, and Mum and I came home from the hospital to an empty house and a shattered future. Later in the evening, there was a knock at the door. Aunt Ethel had travelled miles to be with us. She said very little but she was there; words couldn't help just then, but her presence spoke louder than words—she loved us and cared for us. Comment three explains how we felt and what she did for us:

> "Hope can be ignited by a spark of encouragement."

And the fourth comment also underlines the importance of family and friendship:

> "When we feel the strength of the storm we learn the strength of the anchor."

Family, friendships, faith-strength for life for all of us. My Aunt was there when we needed her, and, yes, as the years went by she always was. Consider comment five:

> "When all you have is God, you have all you need!"

God has made a covenant with humanity. He has promised, "*I will be with you*" (Matthew 28:20). For all of us there are times when we feel empty of hope and happiness. The future looms too large for us to cope with. So comment six is valuable advice: "Don't tell God how big your giants are—tell your giants how big your God is!" A perfect conclusion to comments 1,2,3,4,5, and 6 is the seventh and last: *"The light of the world knows no power cut!"* Let's thank God for that!

Surplus to Requirements?

I recollect an event, in another part of the UK, and several years ago, when parents and children were climbing onto a coach for a day out at the sea side. Suddenly, "they" arrived—a family who didn't belong to the group and who had not signed up for the outing. The organiser barred their way and said, "Sorry, you didn't sign the list and there is no room for you!" The coach door closed and the journey began. I still remember the forlorn faces of those children who were not included—and I guess they remember the occasion as well.

Looking at the media's portrayal of the groups of immigrants who were not allowed to board a train in Budapest, I had a similar reaction. However their future pans out, they will not forget how it feels to be surplus to requirements. The image of the 3 year old boy, washed up on the beach by a callous tide like a piece of rubbish will likewise be forever a part of our memory.

The future is founded on episodes like this—on such memories civilisations can flounder and fail. But what can we do about it? We are ordinary people, living in a green and pleasant valley in Wales. We are not politicians, we are not millionaires—our influence is abundantly limited by situation and circumstances.

Now, it might sound presumptuous, pious and even pedantic to suggest prayer as a practical way of addressing a condition which is out of control. But positive prayer is the only weapon we have to combat man's inhumanity to man.

The Christian faith dares to identify that there might be calamity and catastrophe; but through it all, there is always God. The Bible declares:

"Who, then, can separate us from the love of Christ? Can trouble do it, or hardship or persecution or hunger or poverty or danger or death? … No, in all these things we have complete victory through him who loved us! For I am certain that nothing can separate us from his love: neither death nor life, neither angels nor other heavenly rulers or powers …" (Romans 8:35-38)

No one is surplus to God's requirements. For the sake of the whole of humankind, we need to remember that truth!

This Soap is Good!

We met a gentleman in Africa who told us, "There is only one thing I cannot provide for myself! My food grows or I catch it. I built my house with the materials I found in the forest. The river washes me and my clothes—but to get really clean, I need SOAP."

I have a memory of arriving late one evening at a Missionary Compound to be greeted by the Watchman, who was taking the opportunity to wash in the river. He rose up out of the water, covered in white soapy bubbles. "This soap is good!" he said.

We take soap for granted. It comes in all colours, fragrances, degrees of oiliness, sizes, and shapes. Its one purpose is to make us clean. This is an adequate description of religion!

Religion is a system which is presented in a number of different ways with the one purpose: to make us clean. Humanity's grubbiness can be described in various words but one word suffices for all the others. That word is Sin.

Sin disfigures every society, and every single soul. All faiths have one intention: to clean up humanity and appease a righteous God. But how can human effort appease God? How can sinful man deal with his own sinfulness?

The Christian faith provides the only answer! God placed Jesus on planet earth to identify with humanity. When Jesus was crucified he paid the penalty for the sin and guilt of the entire human race. When we identify with Jesus he cleans us up.

Faith in Jesus is heavenly soap! A convicted prisoner, in a maximum security jail, put it like this "When I accepted Jesus as my Saviour, I was still inside—but inside, I was clean."

On the first Easter Day Jesus rose from the dead, and this indicates that God accepted his sacrifice. Personal Spring cleaning is available through faith in Jesus Christ.

We all need to pray: "Remove my sin, and I will be clean; wash me, and I will be whiter than snow." (Psalm 51:7)

Mountains of Safety

Our Welsh mountains are magnificent in Spring. They are green and beautiful, lovely in the early morning light and majestic in the crimson and gold of a shepherds' delight sunset. They remind me of a very old story which unfolds as follows.

There was a war between Syria and Israel. Numbers were on the side of Syria but in Israel there was a prophet named Elisha, who seemed to have a hotline to Heaven. The story reads like this: when the King of Syria would confer with his officers and say, "We will mobilize our forces at such and such a place," Elisha the man of God would warn the King of Israel not to go near that place because the Syrians were planning to be there.

The King of Syria resolved to deal with the situation by removing Elisha, so one night he sent a great array of troops, horses, and chariots to surround the city where Elisha lived in order to capture him.

Elisha's servant got up early the next morning. He went outside to enjoy the beauty of the pearly light on the mountain slopes. Then he looked down into the city and saw the Syrian army! He rushed to alert Elisha. How did Elisha react? He calmly said:

""Don't be afraid …. We have more on our side than they have on theirs." Then he prayed, "O LORD, open his eyes and let him see!" (2 Kings 6:16–17)

The servant looked up and saw that the hillside around them was filled with horses and chariots of fire!

I once told this story to a group of children in a school assembly in Blaenavon. As I reached the climax, with the Hosts of God in place on the mountain slopes, every head turned towards the window to see if the same presence surrounded their own town. The prayer in every valley church is that God will open our eyes to identify His unfailing, unceasing presence around the people on planet earth.

Our mountains are an unfailing memory prompt to the fact that Gods promise, *"Surely I will be with you,"* will never be broken. Remember—don't look down; look up!

Easter Egg Time

When Easter comes and the shops ooze with chocolate extravaganza, my memory recollects an Easter feast prepared in an African village. The cooking pot contained roast monkey! I had seen the monkeys for sale in the local market, lying amongst other meat—unskinned with their arms carefully folded across their chests. Unrecognisable now it was jointed and well cooked, the savoury smell did not make my mouth water, rather it brought tears to my eyes. I felt more like a cannibal than a carnivore.

On another Easter in rural America, friends were visiting an Indian family. "We have a special treat for you," announced their host. He lifted his gun from a stand in the hallway and said, "I'll just go and shoot two fat squirrels—have you ever tasted squirrel stew?" Don't worry, our local squirrels are safe! My hall stand holds hats and coats rather than guns!

I saw a photo in a newspaper recently which showed 1000 Easter eggs which were to be given away to local children, and this prompted a question. What is so special about an Easter egg? There are so many different sizes, shapes, and fillings, but why celebrate Easter with an egg? Every Easter egg is symbolic in three ways. First, at Easter we remember that Jesus died and was buried. But on the third day after his death, the grave was broken open to let him out. As we break open an Easter egg we are releasing the sweet life which is inside.

Secondly, Easter eggs sometimes contain sweet surprises. Ever since Jesus strode out of his cave tomb on Easter Sunday, he has sweetened the world with his risen presence.

Thirdly, the only way to appreciate an Easter egg is to taste it and see for yourself! I'm not offering you roast monkey or squirrel stew, and I'm not giving away Easter eggs. What I am trying to do is recommend to you the real and glorious truth of Easter. Jesus died and rose again for you that you might have eternal life. In Psalm 34 there is this advice: "Oh, taste and see that the LORD is good! Blessed is the man who takes refuge in him!" (Psalm 34:8 ESV)

Find out the goodness of the Lord for yourself! Ministry is available for you at your local church—why not go along and see?

Remember Jesus

When Jesus was betrayed, tried, condemned to death, and crucified it was a very public occasion. It was Passover time, when the Jews celebrated the memory of their exodus from captivity in Egypt. In the book of Exodus we read:

"And you shall observe the Feast of Unleavened Bread, for on this very day I brought your hosts out of the land of Egypt. Therefore you shall observe this day, throughout your generations, as a statute forever." (Exodus 12:17 ESV)

Every man living within 15 miles of Jerusalem was expected to celebrate Passover in the city; so it would have been crowded with more than 2 million Jews. Notice the publicity of the ride into Jerusalem on a donkey, and the public nature of the crucifixion. Now consider the words of Jesus, as he celebrated Passover feast with his disciples.

St Luke reports that Jesus said, *"I have earnestly desired to eat this Passover with you before I suffer…. Do this in remembrance of me."* (Luke 22:15, 19 ESV) How could Jesus possibly be forgotten? But, unfortunately he often is. I want to note Jesus's request, "Remember me," in four ways.

First—remember, that he enjoys our company! Just as he eagerly desired to be with his friends as he ate the last supper with them, so he enjoys, anticipates, and actually seeks out our company. He is recorded as having said, *"You are my friends,"* and, *"I chose you,"* (John 15:14, 16). This was the last supper that Jesus would eat on earth; the next big event was to be his death. For all of us, the only real certainty in life is that one day we will die.

Secondly, remember his companionship in the evening. Make certain that you have the blessed assurance of his saving and keeping friendship before you do take your last breath. Take to heart the words of Jesus which St John recorded in his gospel: *"And after I go and prepare a place for you, I will come back and take you to myself, so that you will be where I am"* (John 14:3)

The third thing to remember is his compassion. Jesus was betrayed to his enemies by Judas, who was also at the last supper. Jesus knew what Judas was going to do, for he said, *"But, look! The one who betrays me is here at the table with me!"* (Luke 22:21)

But even so, with genuine love, Jesus did not identify Judas by name.

Marvel at the grandeur of his love; hands that flung stars into space, to cruel nails surrendered. Those creative hands which fashioned all that has ever been made were wrecked by Roman hammers as he died that we might be forgiven; that we might go at last to heaven, saved by his precious blood. He himself described that willing sacrifice with these words. He said, "My blood is poured out for you!" Be amazed by such lavish love!

The fourth request to remember is this: Remember the King is coming again. Jesus wore a crown of thorns when he was crucified. He died and was buried in a borrowed tomb. But death could not hold him. On the third day he rose again!

St Luke affirms "Then the Son of Man will appear, coming in a cloud with great power and glory. When these things begin to happen, stand up and raise your heads, because your salvation is near." (Luke 21:27–28)

And—maybe—he could return tomorrow. Are you ready for his coronation day?

My Childhood Dreams

My childhood dreams! Blonde curly hair
A dress of shimmering satin to wear
At a party, with Shirley Temple as guest—
But one dream stood out from all of the rest.

The years from 5 to 11 were the time
When I dreamed of dancing in a pantomime!
Alhambra Theatre, whatever the story,
Featured 12 little girls in stage struck glory.

In that dancing troupe was there room for me ?
But the years went by! It was not to be.
That dream slipped away. Then, as I grew older
Imagination shaped dreams that were bolder.
Myself, centre stage- myself, intended

To gather applause, as my future extended.
Self-satisfaction? Is that a good scheme?
Might that bring life sour milk, instead of rich cream?
Life's like a pantomime. We're on the stage
United together whatever our age.

Keeping in step with the music we hear
Dancing in team with a purpose sincere.

Consider my first dream. Those children were clever-
They enhanced centre stage by working together.

© Antony Rufus | Dreamstime.com

The Squirrels in our Garden

The squirrels who visit our garden have energetic appetites! With agile skill they overcome the construction of squirrel-proof feeders and quickly empty the nuts. They have denuded a miniature apple tree, and it is amusing to watch them swing on the branches to dislodge the tiny green fruits. The fact that the squirrels go on to hide their bounty is proved by the number of little trees growing in unusual places all around our garden!

A scientific magazine contained information that squirrels plant 17,000 trees per acre by forgetting the nuts they have buried! This, of course, might seem like lack of memory on the part of squirrels, but it may also testify to the wisdom of God who utilises the animal's forgetfulness in order to provide them with a better harvest in all the years to come! As the Bible declares:

"We know that in all things God works for good with those who love him, those whom he has called according to his purpose," (Romans 8:28).

When we visited Israel, the enthusiastic guide who met us in Jericho pointed to a large old tree and announced, "This is the tree which Zacchaeus climbed in order to see Jesus." Probably this was a tourist exaggeration, but there is no doubt that centuries ago seeds from a sycamore would have continued the preservation of sycamore trees in Jericho! Just as great oaks grow from single acorns so sycamore keys carry generations of production between their wings.

The lively activity of a baby squirrel in our town has the potential to produce an oak tree which might tower over our valley for centuries. The small man who climbed into a tree one day in order to see Jesus has been remembered on account of this action for more than 2000 years! The mighty potential of small actions is amazing.

As I look across our valley, so verdant with a multitude of trees, I remember that Jesus was a carpenter. He appreciated the strength and beauty of wood. I recollect a couplet I once learned: *"Then those kind hands that did such good—They nailed them to a cross of wood!"*

This single action of crude cruelty has resulted in a munificence of blessing all over the world! In an incredible way the barbarity of the crucifixion produced the largesse of Easter morning. Yet again the Bibles acclamation is verified: *"In all things God works for good with those who love him."*

Autumn Leaves

There are more fallen leaves this year than there were last year—that is, if my memory serves me right! Maybe the quantity of leaves in this Autumn equates with the length and loveliness of summer days or the depth of snow in winter; distance lends enchantment, memory can exaggerate reality.

Is this why we can idealise those good old days? We forget how cold it was without central heating or how long the cold dark evenings were with only the light programme or the third programme for company. And that was only if we had remembered to get the accumulators charged, without which the radio could not even crackle. We had no TV then!

It is important that we remember with accuracy. When a person is brought to trial on evidence concerning an event which took place many years ago, how certain are they about what is said, on oath, to have taken place? We colour the past with the palette of the present. In a meeting the other day we were reminiscing about the "good old days," when churches were full and every child went to Sunday school. Now churches are poorly attended, many have closed down, and very few children go to Sunday school. It seems that God has been forgotten.

Yet social life has definitely not improved! Any TV programme or daily newspaper produces a sequence of avarice, greed, violence, cruelty pain, panic, and political injustice which, to quote someone, "Would make my Grandma blush!"

Everything is falling around us, like all these autumn leaves. The obvious thing to do with falling leaves is to sweep them up and get rid of them! Worship, praise and prayer are good sweeping brushes! The Bible advises,

" First of all, then, I urge that petitions, prayers, requests, and thanksgivings be offered to God for all people; for kings and all others who are in authority, that we may live a quiet and peaceful life with all reverence toward God and with proper conduct. This is good and it pleases God our Savior," (1 Tim 2:1–3).

The palette of this present does not enhance the past when, as a nation, we took time to remember God.

Thanksgiving

Thanksgiving Day is celebrated, in America, on the 4th Thursday of November. I want to share with you one of the legends which surround that day. The voyage which those Pilgrim Fathers embarked upon, from Great Britain to America was long and dangerous. The native Indians fought ferociously to keep their territory.

The Pilgrims' strong faith in God, which had prompted their journey, inspired them to cope in difficult circumstances—and in each small community they built a wooden church in which to pray and praise their God. In one particular service, the Preacher began to read from Psalm 91. *"I will say to the LORD, 'My refuge and my fortress, my God, in whom I trust.' ... He will cover you with his pinions, and under his wings you will find refuge; his faithfulness is a shield and buckler. You will not fear the terror of the night, nor the arrow that flies by day,"* (Psalm 91:2–5 ESV)

At that moment, the door of the church opened violently and in stalked a company of Indians, in war paint and carrying raised tomahawks, ready to chop and kill. They surrounded the small group of worshippers.

Undaunted, the Preacher raised his hand and said, "Let us pray!" His congregation fell on their knees, not knowing if they would ever rise up again. Their Preacher prayed for them, for their new country, and for the guests who had joined them, dressed and equipped as if for a celebration! Then he told his people to stand up and face the Indians. Addressing the chief, he said, "Friends, you are welcome here. Peace be to you." He bowed to them and motioned to his people to do the same.

The Indian chief indicated to his men to lower their tomahawks and then he bowed to the Preacher. He pulled a long white feather from his head dress and fixed it over the doorway. "Your peace!" he said, and quietly those Indians filed out of the church. They never returned.

In all the controversy of the years that followed, that settlement remained under the feather of protection and was left in peace. There is power in prayer! Consider this verse from the Bible:

"Be persistent in prayer, and keep alert as you pray, giving thanks to God." (Colossians 4:2)

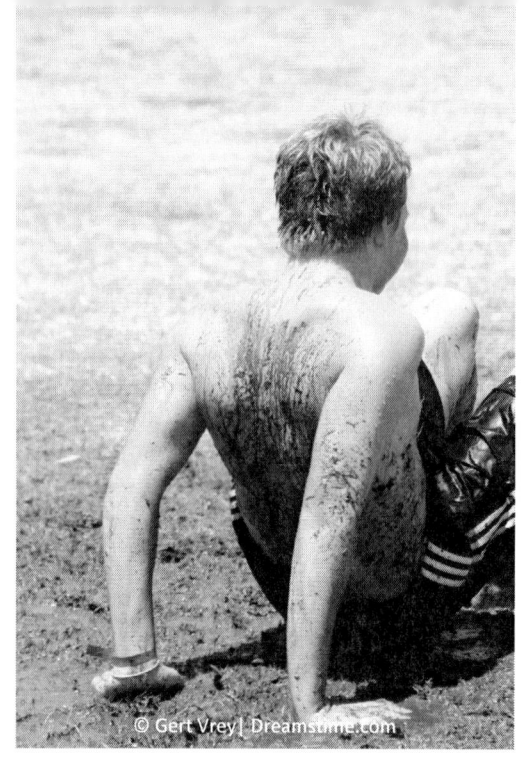

Glorious Mud

On a day when the poetic description of "season of mists" was particularly suitable, we visited Westonbirt Arboretum, near Bristol. The amazing variety, age, height, and colours of the trees were actually enhanced by the misty atmosphere. We were entranced by the blaze of scarlet maple, the pale lemon of sycamore, other leaves of crimson, burgundy, amber, ochre, bronze—a kaleidoscope of colour against the background of a grey misty sky.

There were many families also visiting the Arboretum. We laughed as a little toddler discovered a very muddy puddle. He bounced into it, slipped—and discovered the experience of "mud, mud, glorious mud!" In one glade there was a huge statue of Gruffalo—a frightening character in a children's story book. A child in a push chair saw it, fell out of his chair in excitement and crawled across to touch the ominous feet—in the mud!

At this point I remembered a holiday in Austria! There such a glade would be blessed with a small and tasteful way-side shrine, a delightful reminder of the Author of creation. Such a reminder, "all things bright and beautiful, the Lord God made them all," added to the loveliness of the scenery! It does seem at times as if mankind prefers to muddle in the mud! However, I did not notice any adults sitting in puddles or embracing Gruffalo feet!

Maybe society needs to grow up and acknowledge the greatness of God! Every glowing leaf is an affirmation of God's promise to Noah, "As long as the earth remains there will be seedtime and harvest, cold and heat, day and night, summer and winter."

The young boy's dad was quick to lift his son out of the mud, and in the same way our Heavenly Father is close to us each time we slip and fall. Consider this Bible verse:

"I waited patiently for the LORD; he inclined to me and heard my cry. He drew me up from the pit of destruction, out of the miry bog, and set my feet upon a rock, making my steps secure."(Psalm 40:1–2 ESV)

Surely we prefer God to a Gruffalo? Remember these words:

"Oh give thanks to the LORD, for he is good, for his steadfast love endures forever!" (Psalm 107:1 ESV)

Bring on the Rain

The month of November in Britain has sometimes been incredibly warm—more like spring than late autumn! This is verified by the growth in gardens and the behaviour of birds and little animals. In warm years there have been reports of apple trees coming into blossom in November, animals such as hedgehogs delay their hibernation and birds that should have migrated, remain in the country during the shortening days. Even the grass continues to grow, although because of the rain it stays too wet to be cut!

I read a delightful report about the heavy rain which has deluged many areas of the world including in Wales. Recently a storm came from the Pacific and unleashed the heaviest rainfalls in nearly 100 years on part of the Atacama Desert in Chile. The freak rains triggered an astonishing bloom of flowers.

Plant seeds which had been buried for years burst into life and carpeted the desert in pink, orange, yellow, and purple flowers!

I was reminded of this verse from the Bible: *"The wilderness and the dry land shall be glad; the desert shall rejoice and blossom like the crocus; it shall blossom abundantly and rejoice with joy and singing."* (Isaiah 35:1–2 ESV)

We watch TV, survey the media, and ask ourselves, "Whatever is wrong with humanity?" The landscape of living looks as barren and parched as any desert. Consider this Bible verse *"I will send victory from the sky like rain; the earth will open to receive it and will blossom with freedom and justice. I, the LORD, will make this happen."* (Isaiah 45:8)

Rain brings refreshment, encourages growth, promotes beauty, clears away dirt and debris, and by replenishing rivers and reservoirs, provides for the future.

The showers of God's blessings are refreshing, beautifying, encouraging growth in grace, goodness and wisdom! They ensure all our future. The card shops display Christmas cards depicting snowmen, Santa Claus, holly, rosy breasted robins, angels, starry skies, parties, all with spangles and sparkles. Maybe a card with rain and a rainbow over the stable would strike a new note? When Jesus was born, God's righteousness was showered on earth, so that the beauty of His original plan and purpose might blossom again. With this image in mind, don't put an umbrella on your Christmas list! Allow God's blessings to drench you.

Christmas Joy

December! The nostalgic month! Family traditions, the tree and the trimmings, letters from people whom we only contact once a year—all come in December. Turkey, mince pies, and for those of us who cheerfully disregard health and safety on this occasion—Christmas pudding with silver sixpences hidden amongst the sultanas and raisins. Christmas is a time of sharing together, family and friends can enjoy each other's company and retell those stories of Christmas past, which outrival anything which Charles Dickens wrote!

With each repetition, memory shines brightly and fellowship is richer for the remembering. There is an anecdote which I relocate each Christmas. A small girl hurried home from school and said to her Mum, "I'm a cornflake in the Christmas concert and you've got to dress me in bright yellow!" Mum was rather doubtful, but the child insisted she was going to be a cornflake—so Mum and Gran set to work and produced a glorious, bright yellow costume for the occasion. Came the afternoon of the concert, and onto the stage skipped—a troop of white snowflakes and one radiant yellow cornflake! I am grateful for the mistake!

One cornflake made a great impact! And one radiant person amongst any concentration of cold situations and circumstances will also make a noticeable difference I unpack this story with real pleasure. For me, it epitomises what God purposed to do when He placed His glory into the human body of Baby Jesus. He came, to save his people from their sins. He is Immanuel, God with us.

The present Christmas will become Christmas past when the calendar changes into next year. The tree, trimmings, turkey bones, cards, debris—all removed Silver sixpences will be washed and stored away for another 12 months. Weather forecasts might weaken our resolve to walk off the extra weight of all those festive meals! But memory lives on.

We can identify with the chorus, "Shine, Jesus, shine—fill this land with the Father's glory." God's light in our living can brighten up every day. Jesus is not just for Christmas. He is a living, bright reality.

"Be still, and know that I am God. I will be exalted among the nations, I will be exalted in the earth!" (Psalm 46:10 ESV)

Chinese Whispers

Chinese whispers—where people pass messages to each other by whispering them into the ear of the next person, resulting in a changed message at the end of the line—can have amusing results. A classic is a message sent in wartime, "Send reinforcements, we are going to advance," became, "Send three and four pence, we are going to a dance!"

It is a fact that people do not always listen properly to what is being said. What we think we hear can be translated by our own expectation of what is being said, by the perception of our own thoughts and desires. How did the original statement become so different? Maybe it was because the original message was delivered in a whisper. The Bible which advises: "Clap your hands, all peoples! Shout to God with loud songs of joy! For the LORD, the Most High, is to be feared, a great king over all the earth." (Psalm 47:1–2 ESV)

Perhaps the great, liberating fact of God, the maker of heaven and earth, is being whispered about rather than proclaimed as an adamant truth! Whispers do not disturb, alarm or necessarily provoke any response from people at all. Certainly, if there is danger, a shout would be a better way to issue a warning. The third verse in the entire Bible—and there are 31,102 verses altogether—tells us, "God said 'Let there be light' and there was light." (Genesis 1:3 ESV)

I heard a broadcast this morning concerning the actual beginnings of the Universe, and attempting to define the Big Bang which began it all. The fact that God didn't raise his voice when He created all things emphasises His glory and certainly gives humanity something to shout about. Consider this description: "The voice of the LORD is heard in all its might and majesty" (Psalm 29:4). God doesn't need to shout to make His presence known, God SAID "Let there be light!" His authority is such that He did not need to raise his voice.

The message proclaimed in any church is certainly proclaimed in wartime! Even a casual glance at any newspaper or TV programme will identify the battle between right and wrong. The grace and goodness of God is priceless, but we will want to dance with delight when we really listen to Him! Faith is not a game to whisper about - it is an amazing fact!

The Birthday Cake

My grandson baked a cake for my birthday. It was a recipe for a chocolate cake and he added extra chocolate so that the resulting cake was an extravagance of opulence! When we cut it, to the family chorus of Happy Birthday to you, it slid apart into sections of sweet, creamy slices which were an epitome of indulgence. "Grandma," he said, "You deserve the best."

It is a sad fact that society today tends to under value old age. Election manifestos discuss the cost of the NHS and welfare provision and express concern at the increasing responsibility to the nation of the number of old people who will require extra care. But what a privilege it is for a nation to have elderly citizens. The two world wars diminished population in the UK.

In other countries right now there are fewer old people because of political crises. In the UK we do not suffer the trauma of mass graves concealing the slain bodies of young men who fell into rebel hands, and so will never grow old...

We should respect our elderly people, and encourage the younger generation to do so as well. Our history is stored in their memories—and just maybe their memories will remain vibrant and active because we allow them the exercise of retelling the events which fashioned their lives and created our living!

For instance, although the local "Fowlers" department store closed many years before I came to live in the town of Pontypool, by the frequent reminiscences of various friends, it has achieved—for me—the eminence of a small Welsh version of Harrods!

Never say, "I've heard that old story before—just change the channel!" Allow your elderly friend the privilege and gift of your continuing attention. The Bible declares:

"Wisdom is with the aged, and understanding in length of days," (Job 12:12 ESV). The next verse explains, *"With God are wisdom and might; he has counsel and understanding."* (Job 12:13 ESV)

It is an amazing fact that God considers we deserve His best and when we apply to Him, in faith, with trust, He blesses us with a love and care which are truly opulent!

Popping Corks

"What's that noise?" we asked, as we heard irregular popping sounds which we later identified as acorns dropping on the patio slabs. I recollected another occasion when our attention was attracted by an irregular popping sound. Many years ago, when my husband was called to The Bar, there was a reception afterwards and the noise there was the irregular popping of champagne corks! We are teetotal so it was a new sound to us. The dictionary defines noise as: "a sound, especially one that is loud or disturbing." Noise is expected to make an impact on the hearer.

Consider the popping of those acorns. Positive reactions could be: 1. The oak tree has done well this year, 2. Local squirrels will enjoy the feast, 3. I can hear those pops—so I'm not deaf, 4 The Bible promise is affirmed in my back yard: *"As long as the earth remains there will be seedtime and harvest, cold and heat, summer and winter, day and night!"* Consider the popping of the champagne corks:

1. Our nation still celebrates with those who spend their time and energy in promoting justice and righteousness!

2. Our nation still allows individuals to express their different beliefs! No one made any adverse comment on our small array of coke bottles!

3. Of course, it is possible to celebrate without champagne! The Bible goes in for joyful exuberance, as it says: *"Sing to the LORD, all the world! Worship the LORD with joy; come before him with happy songs!"* (Psalm 100:1–2)

Noise attracts attention. The conglomerate of noise concerning the present refugee crisis does not go unnoticed. We cannot close our ears, hearts and minds to the desperate sound of a situation in which people seem to be surplus to requirements.

Prayer always prevails but for it to do so we have to pray! This Bible verse is full of hope for the immigrant people: "The LORD will keep your going out and your coming in from this time forth and forevermore." (Psalm 121:8 ESV)

The noise which started the entire universe is described as "The Big Bang!" The Bible records it like this*: "God said, Let there be light—and there was light."* (Genesis 1:3) Never underestimate the mighty noise of the unfailing love and care of Almighty God.

Garden Wildlife

As the abundance of acorns increases, so do the squirrels in our garden! Even in the rain there were a few bedraggled animals foraging for winter supplies. Does this natural phenomenon portend a bleak winter? Do squirrels understand the forthcoming weather more than the forecasters, their computers and satellites? Time will tell.

A friendly robin surveyed the furry activity from a low branch. His full song and fiery breast were brilliant for autumn, but his full throated October song was a defiant defence of his territory.

Our valley celebrates choral music, but when robins sing to other robins it is a battle cry. When another robin appears in the garden, we enjoy the music but to the intruder it sounds a warning; "Keep out! Trespassers will be dealt with!" The bright red breast is like threatening war paint. Be ready for a fight!

I read an interesting article in which an ornithologist described how he put a stuffed robin, with the red breast inked out, and also some red breast feathers, hung on a piece of wire, both together in a robins territory. The robin ignored the bird without a red breast—but attacked the red breast without a bird!

The Bible gives this definition of war: *"Where do all the fights and quarrels among you come from? They come from your desires for pleasure, which are constantly fighting within you. You want things, but you cannot have them, so you are ready to kill; you strongly desire things, but you cannot get them, so you quarrel and fight."* (James 4:1–2)

Nations rising up against nations has become an accepted if unfortunate fact of history. As time elapses, the fact can be that some actions were based on assumptions—red breast without a bird and the adage, "Act in haste and repent at leisure!" is accurate yet again. When faced with yet another day's doleful dose of political crises and the immensity of immigration intrusions we could be silenced by the potential peril of these problems. However, take note of the Bible advice: *"The prayer of a good person has a powerful effect."* (James 5:16)

That advice surely deserves singing about!

The Wet Sunshine

There are some summers when the sale of sun cream and ice cream vies with the sales of umbrellas and wellingtons! Rainfall is described in various ways: "it's raining cats and dogs," "it's bucketing it down" or "it's coming down in stair rods"—and quite a delightful one; "there's wet sunshine again!"

Whatever we do or say, rain will fall. It is wise to be philosophical about this weather, and make the best of all we have. The dictionary defines a philosopher as someone who is calm and stoical especially in the face of difficulties and disappointments.

So you've lost your umbrella? Chances are that someone has left theirs behind in your hallway; ready for such a downpour as this! To make the best of ALL that we have includes an awareness of the abundance of comforts which we often take for granted. We have a plethora of umbrellas—we have clothes to change into if we do get wet—our homes are warm and dry—we have wages and pensions and we can replace lost umbrellas! Rain washes our streets, waters our gardens, replenishes our reservoirs and you can only see a rainbow if there has been a downpour of rain! A memorable holiday does not depend on place, weather, food, facilities, opportunity to relax and enjoy something different; it is the people we are with who make this a special time! Why, then, are our hopes so often stymied by a bit of "wet sunshine?"

Let the paraphrase "wet sunshine" become acceptable as a replacement for "devastating downpour," "torrential torrent" or "ruinous rainfall"! Choice of words can expand meaning. Consider these Bible paraphrases of words from Psalms:

"The Lord reigns for ever," becomes, "God holds the high corner." "The Lord is righteous "becomes "God's business is putting things right," and "God is at my right hand, I will not be shaken " becomes "I've got a good thing going and I'm not letting go!"

Remember, God sends the snow in winter, the warmth to swell the grain, the breezes and the sunshine AND soft, refreshing rain. So thank the Lord, for all His love. Enjoy the wet sunshine! It won't last for ever.

Keep the Rules

We all have a collection of historical and often hysterical anecdotes which are reassembled and retold on various occasions. The World Rugby Cup gave our family the acceptable opportunity to refresh the memory of my cousin Jim's first, and final (!) appearance as a professional Rugby player.

We all turned out to watch the game. His mother wore a new hat for the event, and carried an umbrella in case it rained and her new head gear got wet. The game began. Energy levels were high.

Jim was tackled. He disappeared under a muscular mob from the other team. His Mam leaped to her feet. She charged onto the pitch, umbrella ready. "They're killing my boy! They're killing my boy!" she yelled, wielding her umbrella right and left into the melee. It took 4 men to carry her off and Jim left the pitch, as well. The hat was squashed into the muddy field—but the umbrella survived!

We always watch rugby matches with enthusiasm. I am impressed by one aspect which is exemplified in every game. The Referee has but to raise his finger and he achieves an immediate response as burly men move obediently to the Sin Bin. The man in charge has the last word. He who holds the whistle must be obeyed!

Noting the many different nations who were playing against each other in Rugby World Cup, I become wistful for a similar awareness of the rules of the game of life. This aspect of obedience to the man in charge should be observed on a wider field than that of a rugby pitch.

Consider this statement from the Bible:

"Every word of God proves true; he is a shield to those who take refuge in him." (Proverbs 30:5 ESV)

God holds the ultimate whistle. Thousands of years ago, He presented humanity with standard rules which, if observed, will protect and preserve any society. These universal and timeless rules are known as The Ten Commandments. The disastrous finale to Jim's career was due to the fact that my Aunt didn't know the rules of the game. What controversy and catastrophe might be prevented if the Ten Commandments were re-established again?

What's in a Name?

What's in a name? A rose by any other name would smell as sweet! Is this a confirmation of another well-known adage—beauty is in the eye of the beholder? I recollect asking my pupils to bring something beautiful for the nature table. One boy brought a red spotted toadstool! I recoiled in horror and was about to say, "That's poisonous! Wash your hands at once!" when I noticed his face. He was absolutely enthralled by the shape, colour, and spotted symmetry of his gift. It seems we were looking at it through two different personality filters. So I put it in a position where we could admire it from a safe distance.

I discovered a lovely myth concerning the name of the foxglove flower. It is imagined that the fairies—who live at the bottom of the garden—fit the flowers onto the paws of a fox so that he can creep up to the chicken without being heard. A fox has velvet paws, because they are sheathed in foxglove blooms.

The chicken, the owner of the chicken run, the down to earth gardener, the careful parent, the scientist will each have a different reaction to the name! This is a lovely plant, it is poisonous yet its medicinal property saves lives; it contains digitalis. What's in a name? Beauty is in the eye of the beholder!

The Bible describes how Jesus got his name. An angel spoke these words to Joseph, *"Do not be afraid to take Mary to be your wife. For it is by the Holy Spirit that she has conceived. She will have a son, and you will name him Jesus—because he will save his people from their sins."* (Matthew 1:20–21)

The name Jesus means, "The Lord saves." Of course we need saving from our mistakes, from danger, from unhealthy atmospheres, and from political chicanery, but most of all we need to be saved from our sins!

The Bible is adamant when it declares that, *"all have sinned and come short of the glory of God,"* (Romans 3:32 ESV). We look at Jesus through our own personality but we cannot admire him from a safe distance! A rose by any other name might smell as sweet—but Jesus, the rose of Sharon, is unique. God has given no other name under heaven by which we must be saved. So what will you do with Jesus; the choice is yours!

The Old Watch

We have an old watch which is designed to be worn on a heavy chain across the waistcoat of its owner. It has this inscription inside its silver case, "John Harrison 1877". Wind it up each day and it keeps accurate time. Polish the silver case and it shines! Although the presentation and performance are not up to present day standards, the inscription is as perfect now as when it was inscribed 138 years ago. We value the watch because of its inscription. John's name is inscribed on time: this portion of time belonged to him. His CV might read like this "John Harrison owns this portion of time and he is responsible for its accurate and attractive presentation."

Time is the most valuable possession we have. Every morning we have the gift of another 24 hours of time. Consider these wise comments about time: *"Trust in God at all times,"* (Psalm 62:8). At just the right time, God promises to respond to your prayer. I don't know if John Harrison 1877 had any other ambition than to live a quiet, respectable life. This ambition is in the Bible:

"First of all, then, I urge that petitions, prayers, requests, and thanksgivings be offered to God for all people; for kings and all others who are in authority, that we may live a quiet and peaceful life with all reverence toward God and with proper conduct." (1 Timothy 2:1–2)

Faith is our key and prayer is the way we polish and present our living. John Harrisons watch is no longer worn every day as it was intended to be. Today, faith and prayer are also often resigned to a shelf as surplus to present day requirements. When something happens which makes us aware that we are unable to cope with time's demands on us, then we return to the Bibles inscriptions which never change.

How about these words from Psalm 9? *"The Lord is a refuge in Times of trouble."* The next 5 years might seem to rest on the shoulders of the elected Government but the success of any Government requires faith and the daily support of prayer. Note the admonition *"to give thanks for them!"*

More wise advice from another Psalm: *"you hear my voice in the morning; at sunrise I offer my prayer and wait for your answer,"* (Psalm 5:3). There will always be an answer!

The Majesty of God

Today the July sky is covered with clouds. There are showers of rain, proving the old rhyme "hot July brings cooling showers."

I read recently about a bizarre new type of cloud which is close to being recognised by The Cloud Appreciation Society. I am amazed to identify that such a publication exists, along with The International Cloud Atlas; however, with English weather's predomination of cloudy skies, probably both the society and the atlas have plenty of material to consider!

The new type of cloud is named "Asperitas" and it looks rather like a turbulent sea, hanging down from the sky. If we were able to identify Asperitas clouds at times we might decide that our life was just like the cloud formation—about to deluge us with a storm of circumstances against which we had no control. It is at such times that the following quotation is reassuring.

"Just a glance into the universe God has made renews faith in a heart-beat."

When we consider the size of the Universe it is indeed amazing that God is concerned about humanity. We measure universe distance in light years; our year has 365 ¼ days; and a light year equals 6 TRILLION miles.

The Sun is 870,000 miles across and the Earth could fit into the Sun 1 million times. The biggest star in our universe is called Canis Majorus, and the Sun could fit into Canis Majorus 21,000 times and this star may be as many as 5,000 light years away from Earth. A plane would take 50 hours to fly around the world; but if it were possible to fly around Canis Majorus the journey could take 11,000 years!

Such is the majesty of creation—and yet humanity is also marked by majesty. The Bible declares, "So God created human beings, making them to be like himself. He created them male and female," (Genesis 1:27)

Grace is amazing because the immensity of God was contracted to a span when—incomprehensibly—He became man and as Jesus Christ walked and experienced the small life of humanity on planet Earth. Against the background of numbers I have just mentioned, marvel at this one: in Gods reckoning, "Even the hairs of your head have all been counted," (Luke 12:7).

Big Mouth!

Possibly the most appropriate phrase for many personal and social encounters these days is "I opened my big mouth too soon!" Throw away comments can appear in tomorrow's headlines—even royalty are not exempt. This came to mind when I received the following news item from a friend in Japan: "For many Japanese women, having an Ochobo (small and modest mouth) is attractive. In public a large open mouth is considered ugly and rude! Therefore, many women deny themselves the pleasure of taking mouth sized bites of big tasty burgers in order to maintain their good manners!

Japan's Freshness Burger fast food restaurant decided to challenge this convention by providing the "Liberation Wrapper." This is a large paper holder with a photo of a woman's closed mouth, nose and chin printed on the paper. As it covers the lower part of the face it hides the mouth and allows the lady to eat a burger with a wide open mouth, even with juice running down her chin!

This clever invention is a huge success. Within a month after introducing the Liberation Wrapper, sales of Classic burgers to female customers went up by 213 per cent!

To have a small and modest mouth, to carefully choose our words, to think before we speak, is undeniably attractive. However, consider this verse from the Bible:

"People look at the outward appearance but the Lord looks at the heart." What we say should express who and what we are. Here are 4 wise proverbs:

1. "The words of the goodly are a life giving fountain."

2. "The words of the godly are like sterling silver."

3. "The words of the godly encourage many."

4. "The lips of the godly speak helpful words."

To be helpful, wise, encouraging and a valuable asset to the society in which we live infers that we live, move and have our being inside a wrapper of godliness-to be contained within the presence of God himself. A mighty ambition! An essential daily prayer for each one of us is this one.

"Let the words of my mouth and the meditation of my heart be acceptable in your sight, O LORD, my rock and my redeemer." (Psalm 19:14 ESV)

Traffic Jam!

The M5 and the M6 are noted for traffic jams! On a recent journey we were stuck behind a lorry carrying industrial waste, and soon our stop-start progress resulted in the front of the car becoming covered with brown grit and dust. Wind screen wipers, necessary so that we could see where we were going, became clogged with the debris. So, as soon as our snail pace allowed, we turned off into a Service station.

We drove onto the garage forecourt, in search of a car wash. There wasn't one; in fact there was no suitable supply of water for our needs. Then, quite unexpectedly, a man in overalls, carrying a large bucket and a mop, came round the petrol pumps. He noticed our situation and offered to help. He sluiced down our car, with a seemingly inexhaustible supply of water—refused any payment—and sent us on our way again, a bright, shining car, with two very grateful passengers! Now, there are three possibilities for the way our car got cleaned up.

1. The mop man's arrival was a lucky coincidence—the right man at the right time.

2. Having already prayed for travelling mercies, we received merciful help when we needed it!

3. And, of course, there is the promise in the Bible: *"God will put his angels in charge of you to protect you wherever you go,"* (Psalm 91:11).

In another Bible verse we are reminded that, *"Some … welcomed angels without knowing it,"* (Hebrews 13:2). Was the man in overall an angel in disguise sent to help us in our time of need? Which solution to our problem agrees most easily with your philosophy of life? We dress up our concept of angels in flowing robes, with impressive wings. The poet Francis Thompson wrote these verses: "Not where the wheeling systems darken - And our benumbed conceiving soars. The drift of pinions, would we hearken - Beats at our own clay shuttered doors. The angels keep their ancient places - Turn but a stone and start a wing. - Tis you, tis your estranged faces - That miss the many splendored thing!"

Psalm 34 reminds us, *"The angel of the LORD encamps around those who fear him, and delivers them,"* (Psalm 34:7 ESV). Do we always recognise the humanity of heavens helpfulness?

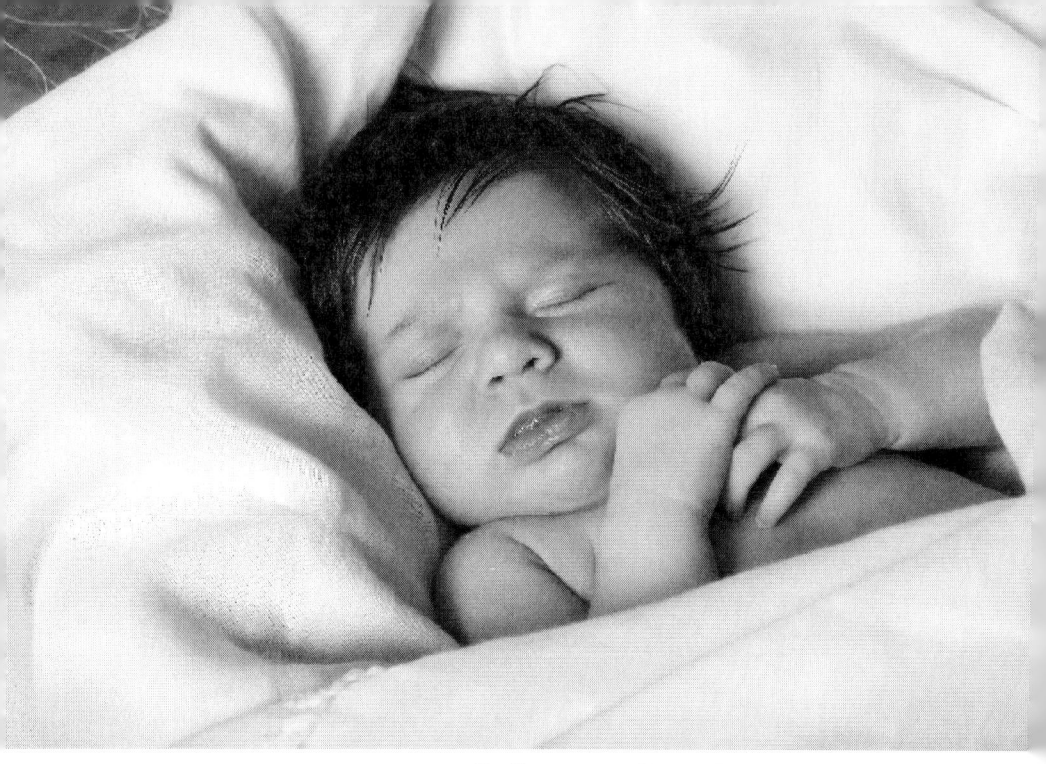

Rejoice and be Glad!

I want to describe Christmas in three short sentences: 1. There was a birth place. 2. There was a birthday party! 3. There were birthday presents. I will refer to the story as Luke has reported it in chapter 2 of his gospel.

First, let's consider the birth place. In those days, Caesar Augustus issued a decree that a census should be taken of the entire Roman world and everyone went to their own town to register. Joseph went from Nazareth to Bethlehem because he belonged to the line of David. Mary, who was pledged to be married to him, was expecting their first child. When they arrived in Bethlehem - there was no room for them in the inn, but they were provided with a stable—there Jesus was born and placed in a manger, for his first cradle.

What a considerate provision of God! In that crowded town, with people enjoying meeting up with friends and relatives—

merrymaking, noise, bustle—God arranged a quiet stable for the birth of Jesus. He provided privacy for the birth and also protection from gossiping tongues; the fact that Mary had testified that this was a virgin conception would have been common knowledge in Nazareth, there would have been prying eyes, to see if the baby had a Roman nose! But God presented them with a safe sanctuary for this wonderful event.

God is always in control. Caesar ordered the census, but God arranged it, so that Jesus birth fulfilled prophecy. The prophet Micah wrote, "Bethlehem Judah, out of you will come one for me who will be ruler over Israel!"

There was a birthday party! The tradition was that when a boy was born, family and friends came to sing to him. And so they did! Luke tells us that a great company of the heavenly host came into the sky over Bethlehem, praising God. This was family, singing with joy for the birth of the son of God. They sang to shepherds in those fields, keeping watch over their flocks through the night. Jesus is the good shepherd—so here were other shepherds, hurrying to the stable to see him on his birthday.

How appropriate that these particular shepherds shared in this unique birthday party. They were looking after the lambs that were destined to be sacrificed in the temple. They rejoiced to see the ultimate Lamb of God - who takes away the sins of the world.

There were birthday presents, too. There was the gift of reassurance when there was no room for them in the inn, can you imagine how Joseph and Mary felt? When they looked at baby Jesus, new born and so very ordinary, just like any other baby - how do you think they felt? Could this really be the son of God? And then—in came the Shepherds with the exciting news of an angel choir singing about a Saviour, who is Christ the Lord, born in the stable behind the inn and lying in a manger.

This was also the gift of rejoicing! Luke writes, "The shepherds returned, glorifying and praising God for the things they had heard and seen which were just as they had been told!"

Rejoice, and be glad—the Redeemer has come!

"I am always aware of the LORD's presence; he is near, and nothing can shake me. And so I am thankful and glad, and I feel completely secure," (Psalm 16:8–9)

Childhood Memory

My cousin's name was James, or Jim,
And we were very proud of him.
With muscles strong, and power like steam,
He was chosen for the Rugby team.

His Mam, my aunt, filled great big plates
With food for Jim and for his mates.
He never did odd jobs, like me,
For he was in the team, you see!

We all turned up to see him play
I had my hair curled for that day!
His Mam, my aunt, wore a fine new hat—
It was trimmed with fur like the back of our cat.

The teams came on, the game began,
They were all in the scrum, piled man on man.
Then up jumped my aunt, she ran on the field,
And a spiked umbrella she did wield

On every head that she could reach.
"Get off my boy, you thugs," she screeched!
Four men came on to carry her out,
That was Jim's first and final bout!

More from Faithbuilders Publishing:

Faithbuilders Bible Study: The Gospel of Matthew

Faithbuilders Bible Study: The Gospel of Mark

The Pentecostal Bible Commentary Series: 1 Corinthians

The Prophet of Messiah

The Blessings of God's Grace

The Message of Mark

The Prophecy of Amos – A Warning for Today

More from Doreen Harrison

A Bouquet of Blessings

Coping with the Wobbles of Life

The Donkey Boy

Jubilant Jeremy Johnson

A Book of Bible Stories